300 YEARS
"DEVOTION TO DUTY"

By Andy Endacott

THE ROYAL ALBERT BRIDGE AT SALTASH.

The choice of Plymouth as a Naval Base was largely due to Sir Francis Drake whose home port was Plymouth and also Sir John Hawkins in the 1500's.

During the reign of Charles I, Saltash had been chosen for a site of a Government Dock in 1625, but had to be abandoned after strong objections against a Naval Base on their sacred soil, which would destroy their fishing industry and livelihood.

Further areas were considered such as the Hamoze, Cattewater and even Dartmouth and estimates sent to the Admiralty in 1689.

As we now realise, a stone dock proposal was accepted and built on the Hamoze and was begun on 2nd September 1691. By the end of 1692 the wet basin and dry dock had been completed. The Navy rented the land used called POINT FROWARD, for an annual fee of £100 for the first seven years, and the work force totalled 74 men. This was to be the beginning of the largest Naval Dockyard in Europe, over a period of 300 years.

THE DOCKYARD

. . . has been described as a Town within a Town. Over its 2 ½ miles length, it has its own bus service, double yellow lines, pedestrian crossings, yellow boxed junctions and to complete the comparison, a police force and its own traffic wardens.

In 1765 the employment of artizans was very extensive including shipwrights, caulkers, joiners, smiths, sawyers, ropemakers, masons, painters, plumbers, riggers, sailmakers, and labourers approaching near 1800; to each class were added apprentices.

Nearly 500 Convicts were also employed as labourers, in various departmentss, making over 2000 men employed, exclusive of those men employed on works executed by contract.

In time of war, the establishment was augmented to about 4000. The sum of £104,000 annually was paid in wages.

A final comparison can be given on numbers, wages and docks.

YEAR	WORK/FORCE	WAGES	DOCKS
1895	4619	£363,197	7
1984	13,600	£120 Million	15

The Author

Born in Plymouth, Devon – Andy Endacott was educated at Devonport High School and entered the Dockyard in 1946 as a Shipwright apprentice.

After 2 years National Service in the R.A.F. as aircrew and on photographic interpretation work, he returned to the Yard in 1953.

Entering the Drawing Office in 1954, doing drawing work for many refits on Air Craft Carriers.

Moved to the Mould Loft in 1970, this time on Model Making projects, both small scale and full size. Eventually retired from the Dockyard in 1990.

A keen racing cyclist, and photographer with his own darkroom, he also started freelance reporting in 1954.

After 1965 became involved with Steam Traction Engines, and consequently wrote 3 Steam Books. and took up commentating at rallies.

Since 1983 found a further interest in collecting Naval Postcards, and documentation on the Dockyard.

Has now written and published 3 volumes of 'Naval Heritage in the West' and gives talks and slide shows on these subjects.

Now retired he hopes to give more time to recording Naval History in the area, for the future generations to read.

Other titles by the same Author, available in bookshops.

Naval Heritage in the West Part II covers 1900-1950
Battleships, Shipbuilding, Naval Colleges, Big Guns, Royal Marines, Wrens, VIP's, early Fleet Air Arm and Famous Ships.

Naval Heritage in the West Part III covers 1940-1987
Dockyard Work, River Activities, End of Many Traditions, Training Establishments, Flash-Back Items, Cadet Corps, RFA's and Operation Corporate.

ISBN 0.9511527.3.4
First Published September 1991
Text © D.L. ENDACOTT 1991

Published by D.L. Endacott, 47 Pounds Park, Saltash, Cornwall PL12 6BT and printed by Penwell Ltd, Parkwood, Callington, Cornwall.

INTRODUCTION

It might not seem the correct time to celebrate a birthday, with a recession and a large number of redundancies taking place, but we cannot alter history. Many of the men that have been made redundant have quickly been re-employed with outside firms, who have recognised the high performance skills these men possess, due to their Dockyard training.

I have endeavoured to cover as much as possible in this book, hoping the reader possesses parts 1, 2 and 3 – Naval Heritage in the West, or has at least seen them. With this in mind I have tried not to repeat the photo's.

It is really an impossible task to cover 300 years in one book when some of the subjects i.e. Building of the Large Dock Complex could be a book in itself. Still, to make the journey interesting I have used prints, drawings and photo's where available at the time.

Many families have had someone who has worked in the Dockyard or served in the Navy. It has been said that nearly 40% of the City of Plymouth's money is from Crown Naval expenditure and wages.

We are going through a very bad period, with World Peace Agreements being actioned, there is again talk of closing another Dockyard. We heard it before in 1929, 1939 and after the Second World War. The Falklands and the Gulf Wars gave the yards increased work. It is a sad fact that many establishments linked with the Armed Forces need a war for their industries to survive, and yet don't really want the horror of it to happen.

It is also very unfortunate since the Second World War, we have advanced with technology too fast in such a short time. Now many industries with these electronics can do with less people. The new Type 23 for example only needs a crew of 157, against last years Type 22 of 250 men. So working people will become redundant under a future electronic world.

Meanwhile, back to earth, let's hope such areas as Royal William Yard and South Yard where Devonport Dockyard started as Plymouth Docks over 300 years ago can be retained for the nation, as living museums and theme areas of our Naval Heritage. Certainly the buildings and docks of Cornish Granite will last another 300 years. Will we see sense as a civilisation to remember our past.

Portsmouth and Chatham, are endeavouring to survive as Naval Theme areas, giving employment. Of course Portsmouth has the advantage of 3 major ship attractions, whilst we still argue about the need for HMS *Plymouth* and a Heritage Area, wake up to the future by using the past as a medium for employment.

Finally I must give special reference should you want to know more details of the yard, to two publications.

'Devonport Dockyard Story' by the late Lt Commander Ken Burns, (available Maritime Books, Liskeard). And 'History of Devonport Dockyard' by the late George Dicker (available Dockyard Curator).

Also visits to the yard can be arranged by appointment.

Acknowledgements

I would like to thank the following for their help in preparing this final photographic history story on the Dockyard:-
Peter Waterhouse, Dave Scoble, Hilary Sibbett (DML Devonport Link – Editor), John Constantine (Devonport Photographic Section), John Rippin – Retired Draughtsman. Finally Chris Conyon, who decoded my pencilled text and converted it to a sensible computer print out and learnt about the Dockyard on route.

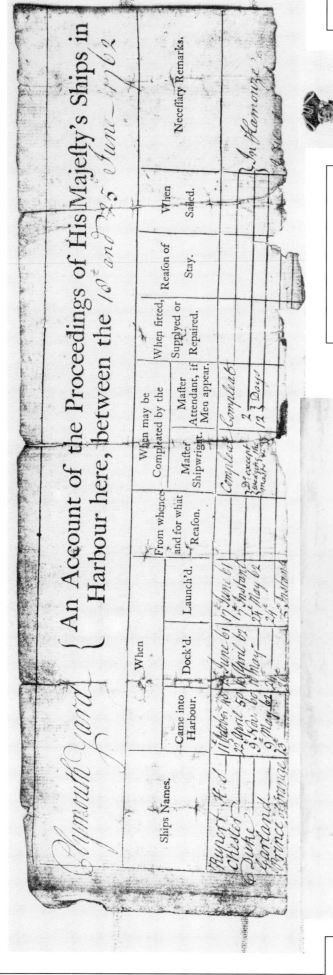

Plymouth Yard { An Account of the Proceedings of His Majesty's Ships in Harbour here, between the 10th and 25 June 1762.

Ships Names.	When — Came into Harbour.	Dock'd.	Launch'd.	From whence and for what Reason.	When may be Completed by the — Master Shipwright.	Master Attendant, if Men appear.	When fitted, Supplied or Repaired.	Reason of Stay.	When Sailed.	Necessary Remarks.
Rupert H.d	1 March 61	1 June 61	17 June 61		Compleat	Compleat				In Hamoaze
Chester	22 April 50	8 April 62	17 Instant	Diexcept the King's the small's		2½ Days				
Duke	9 Nov. 60	22 May 62	24 Instant			12½ Days				
Portland	9 May 62	24th	24th Instant							
Prince of Orange	13		5 Instant							

The ships Boatswain, (circa 1828). This black glazed top hat, and blue double breasted tail coat, with white trousers make up the main uniform. The belt supported a jack knife and sword.

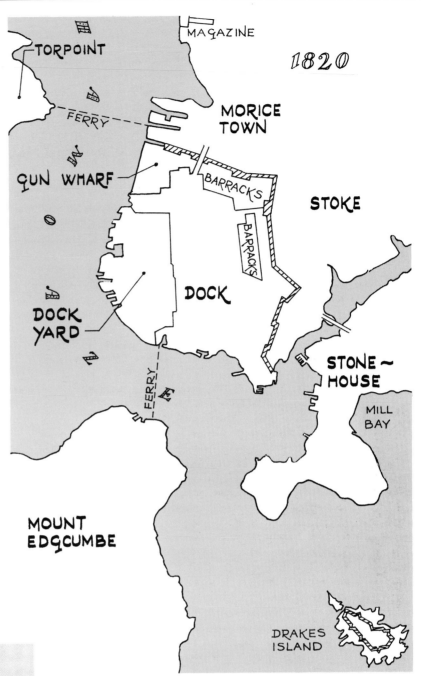

1820

TORPOINT

MAGAZINE

MORICE TOWN

FERRY

GUN WHARF

BARRACKS

STOKE

BARRACKS

DOCK

DOCK YARD

STONE~HOUSE

FERRY

MILL BAY

MOUNT EDGCUMBE

DRAKES ISLAND

The Dockyard has now expanded its area, to include mast ponds, extra docks and the work force was now 2000.

The Battleship *Mars* was built in 1794, it carried 74 guns, and saw action against the French, also assisting in the bombardment of Copenhagen in 1807. This would be the style of ship that would require the use of the Dockyard in the 19th century.

Figurehead of HMS *Bellerophon*. She was a line-of-battle-
ship of 1,613 tons with 74 guns, and in 1815 was used to
transfer Napoleon from Plymouth to St Helena for his exile.

Player's
Cigarettes.

H.M.S BELLEROPHON

HMS *Captivity*. Was originally the *Bellerophon*, renamed in 1824, and converted to a prison ship in 1826, she brought a ship load to the yard to be
employed as labourers. Shown here at her yard berth whilst she continued
as a prison ship until 1836.

Their Royal Highness's the Duchess of Kent, and the Princess Victoria
approach the Kings Steps at Devonport Dockyard on the 2nd of August 1833.
Note the Dockyard Chapel is flying a Royal Welcome Flag.

The original Torpoint Ferry service commenced in 1791 and varied in their construction for many years. The first Torpoint Floating Bridge was introduced by J.M. Rendel in 1834, quote, ".....being a ferry itself acting on chains connecting the two river banks." The sketch in 1870 indicates the view from the Devonport inclined beach, across to Torpoint with the ferries midstream. The Royal Mail coach was taken across without even unhorsing, plus 5 or 6 coaches and foot passengers. The journey took approximately eight minutes and in 1840 the tolls taken amounted to £2,400.

A domestic scene covering the ferry at Torpoint, with numerous wooden walled ships in the river against the background of the Quadrangle with its 2 prominent tall chimneys. Before Torpoint existed, the Navy used to 'careen' their ships on that side of the river. This consisted of laying the ship on its side to allow the seaweed and other accretions to be removed, and then re-tarred before the next high tide. When houses were first built for the dockyard workers on the Cornish side, the area was referred to as Tar Point.

The Great Fire of Sept 1840 in the Dockyard should have a full chapter to be described correctly. It commenced on the *Talavera* and quickly spread to other ships, sheds and stores. Being wooden ships with so much pitch, oakumn and paint about, the fire ran wild. It burnt one shed containing 300 mens tool boxes valued at £7 each. Thirty six fire engines, consisting of Army outfits-floating engines, plus a West of England engine from Plymouth, drawn by four horses. Total damage cost was £80,000.

Mr John Braithwaite produced the first steam fire engine in 1829, but it was not until some 30 years later that steam fire engines came into general use. The Merryweather steamer *Sunderland* won first prize at Crystal Palace in 1863. This engine was then purchased by the Lords of the Admiralty for the protection of Devonport Dockyard. It went out of commission in 1905, and was returned to the makers works, as a fine specimen of the early steam fire engines.

Over the years the Dockyard fire brigade has been manned by the Metropolitan Police, R.N. Fire Force and Royal Marine Police, until disbanded in 1968. It is now covered by the City Brigade.

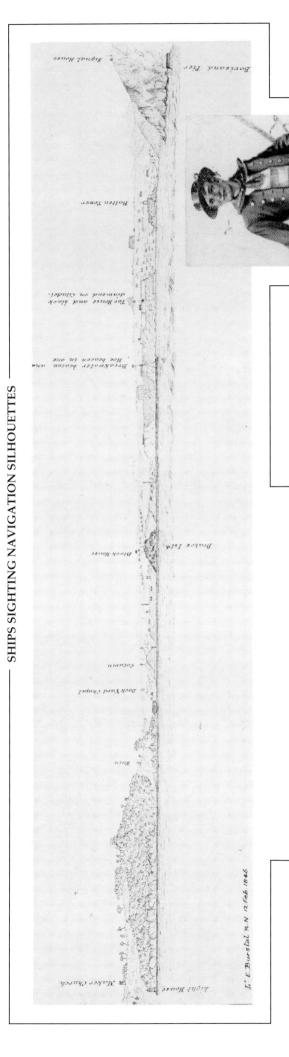

A seaman (circa 1845), now shown wearing the more supple garment of a striped jersey, in blue and white, under a blue waistcoat, and white canvas trousers. The hat was glazed by the seaman, by covering it with paint or tar, and consequently it became thicker and heavier.

During this period of moving from port to port a method was devised for the navigating officer and officer of the watch, to readily be able to identify the various coast lines. These show the approaches to Plymouth Sound, coming from Torbay or down channel past Wembury, then Drakes Island and sightings on the Dockyard Chapel and Batten Tower, which would have been shown on the ships charts.

THE ROYAL WILLIAM VICTUALING YARD.

Royal William Victualling Yard was completed in 1835 and supplied the needs of the old Navy from these buildings, consisting of the cooperage, slaughter house, meat curing, flour mill, biscuit bakery and chocolate mill manufacturers. For instance, in the bakery where bread was made for the Navy, a steam engine and 25 pair of mill stones were capable of grinding 1,000 bushels of corn into meal within 10 hours.

During the 20th century, all the activities were to be changed to obtaining clothing and mess gear for the Navy, and now at the end, even that has stopped. Its future is uncertain, other than it will no longer serve the Navy as designed.

An East India Company's ship of the period using Royal William Yard which was built in the early 19th century. These merchant ships carried arms and were used at times for naval engagements. The Company lost their charter in 1834, and those not broken up were used by the Navy as free traders, transports, or as convict ships.

A warrant officer (circa 1863) shown in a complete blue uniform. The double breasted coat was finished with gilt buttons and offset with a stiff wing collar on the shirt.

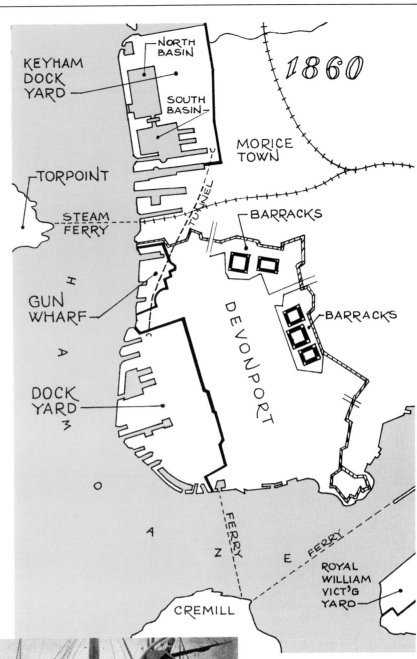

1860

KEYHAM DOCK YARD
NORTH BASIN
SOUTH BASIN
MORICE TOWN
TORPOINT
STEAM FERRY
BARRACKS
GUN WHARF
DEVONPORT
BARRACKS
DOCK YARD
FERRY
FERRY
ROYAL WILLIAM VICT'G YARD
CREMILL

The Dockyard has now increased with the opening of Keyham Dockyard in 1853, by the Queen. HMS *Queen* entered No.7 Dock fully manned on the yard arms and the dock was called 'Queen's Dock' to mark the occasion.

A tunnel connecting the two yards was also constructed and the work force now reached 3,200.

Transport *Jumna* in drydock. An iron screw vessel, she was launched by Lady Margaret Beaumont at Palmer Bros yard Jarrow on September 24th, 1866. She was a member of a group of Government transports which drew the nickname of 'lobster pots' by their general unwieldiness.

Here shown in No.7 Dock, Devonport Dockyard.

HMS *Lion* one of the many Training Ships, a Battleship of 2589 tons, that ended her days at Devonport. Her heaviest gun was a 32 pounder, but there were many of them.

HMS *Implacable* seen here mid stream in attendance with other wooden wallers to end her days as a training ship. She served at the Battle of Trafalgar and became the first Royal Naval Training ship in 1860.

Queens dock was later lengthened 100ft to allow longer vessels such as the armoured ship *Warrior* to dock. Throughout the life of the Dockyard some docks were always being extended to take a particular ship.

The Quadrangle area consisted on the north side of the Boiler Shop, which contained the boiler smiths shop and platers shop. On the east side, iron foundry, pattern shop and brass foundry. South side coppersmiths and blacksmiths shop, with fitting and erecting shops.

KEYHAM YARD 1866

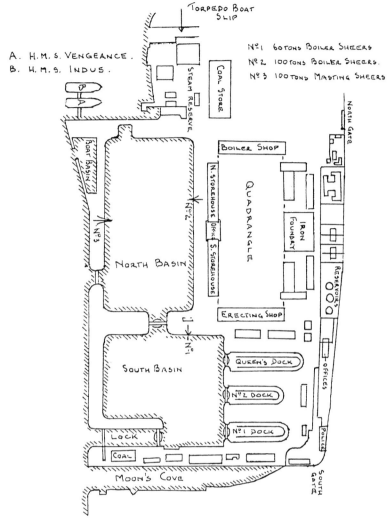

A. H.M.S. VENGEANCE.
B. H.M.S. INDUS.

Nº1 60 TONS BOILER SHEERS
Nº2 100 TONS BOILER SHEERS.
Nº3 100 TONS MASTING SHEERS

The two hulks *Vengeance* and *Indus* with a timber pound in foreground, ready to construct frameworks for the new Keyham Extension (i.e. North Yard). The *Vengeance* had been used by the yard as a receiving hulk and torpedo store for 30 years. When tugs attempted to tow her to the Cattewater she split apart and embedded herself in the mud.

Sir Walter Raleigh was himself an accomplished navigator and one of his cruises formally took possession of Virginia. An incidental result of this being the introduction of tobacco into England. His name has been preserved in the Navy down to the present day.

Illustrated here on a famous occasion in 1899 is the ship-rigged steam frigate HMS *Raleigh* leading the last squadron of the Royal Navy ever to put to sea under sail, consisting of *Volage, Champion* and *Cleopatra*.

It is therefore unfortunate that in the mid 1980's that mass advertising of tobacco was greatly reduced, due to the medical fact established, that tobacco brought back by Raleigh was now responsible for Lung Cancer in both smokers and passive smokers. The insert view – shows the fine figurehead from the ship HMS *Raleigh*, now retained at its namesake naval training establishment near Torpoint, Cornwall.

SENIOR SERVICE
Satisfy

The decorative entrance of Fore Street Gate, the entrance into South Yard. The large pole and container to the left was the Bell Tower, for in and out muster times, and the Chapel tower can be seen to the right. Also on the right is the Police Accommodation and Office Buildings. The actual gate structure hasn't altered, but the main control gates are now in Granby Way. Clocking stations were on the left inside this gate.

This was the second Dockyard Chapel and was opened in 1817, at a cost of £24,000 and capable of seating 2000 people. Each area being allocated for resident officers and families, Navy and military officers, band, choir, sailors and marines. In the tower were six musical bells, a rare expense in those days, unfortunately it was all destroyed in April 1941 during the wartime blitz. Incidentally the Chaplain's salary was £400 per annum.

The Avenue, Devonport Dockyard.

Moving into South Yard further, we pass down through this Avenue of trees, headed by these ships Figureheads, which have since gone. At the bottom you arrive at the residences of the principle officers of the Dockyard, called The Terrace. Of the 13 houses and 2 main offices, only a couple remain at the north end due to bombing in the second World War.

We are now looking from the river back into South Yard.
This is the first wet basin, start of the Dockyard, with the curved gates to the right being the opening to No.1 Dock. On the upper level is the Terrace of officers accommodation, to the left is the Chapel. The lower buildings from the right, were the officers office block and then the joiners shop in 1900. They have since been demolished, and many other uses made of the area.

A domestic river scene (circa 1904) of the Dockyard and its ships, viewed from Mount Edgecumbe. The covered sheds over the slipways can be seen.
The vessel to the right is the *Impregnable*, and the mid one is another training hulk, and the single funnel yacht is HMS *Vivid*.

These naval ratings are from HMS *Impregnable*, who have gone ashore, and climbed grassy banks to train beside the obelisk at Mount Edgecumbe.
Field Guns were also taken ashore for exercises.

THE IMPREGNABLE MAGAZINE

VOL. 2.   **SUMMER 1937.**   **No. 1.**

H. M. S. IMPREGNABLE.

HMS 'Impregnable'
A fine old ship is she.
She trains her boys who finish up
At the bottom of the sea,
She wakes them up each morning
At five three O precise,
And takes them to the Mess Deck
To give them something nice,
Then off they go to clean ship,
To polish all the decks,
To brighten up the brass work
With skill of the other sex.
Then comes a pleasing moment,
When cooks are sounded off,
All hands fall in for breakfast,
With chests out like a 'toff'.
R.S. Cantle

HMS *Ocean* was to be Devonport's first Battleship on No.3 slip, she was launched 5th July 1898 by H.R.H. Princess Louise, after many delays.

This slip had its roof removed in 1896, so open aired shipbuilding had to be experienced by the men. Part the way through, 2 gangs of men went to assist in docking the Battleship *Colossus* and on their return, about 90 feet of the fore end had collapsed (100 tons of work), due to a labourer removing a bolt, before riveting a section had been completed. Finally due to her great weight the slipway had to be lengthened 30ft before launch.

Dockyard workers of all grades going for a lunch break of 90 minutes, having walked for nearly 6 mins up the long slope from the docks below, before reaching these gates.

HMS *Halcyon*, of the Channel Squadron a steel first-class torpedo-gunboat of the Naval Defence Act Programme and was launched in 1895. She was built at Devonport Dockyard and by her displacement was 1,070 tons, length 250ft, beam 30ft 6 ins and maximum draught 9ft. Her speed was 19 knots. The *Halcyon* was commissioned at Devonport in May 1895 as a tender to the Channel Squadron. She carried the pennant of Commander William G. White.

An artist impression of the imposing entrance to Keyham Yard at Albert Road Gate with its twin towers, the left hand one containing the clock. At this stage (circa 1870) the northern end of the yard had not been started, so the river was still peaceful.

Later in 1972, the complete structural area of this fine gate was removed, with the exception of the right hand tower, also the clock was transferred across, but with a new electric movement.

The old weights, etc, have been retained in the Dockyard Museum. The removal of the entrance was due to the building of the New Frigate Complex.

A Chief Engineer Officer (circa 1880). With the change from sail to steam a new type of officer was created. The uniform is a single breasted blue coat with eight buttons, blue trousers and a cocked hat. Rank was denoted with crowns and stars of gold on the fringed epaulettes, also by lace and stripes of purple material on the sleeve cuffs.

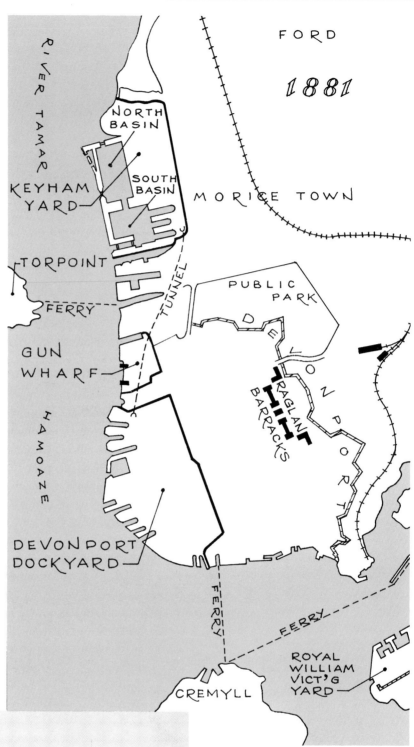

FORD

1881

RIVER TAMAR

NORTH BASIN

KEYHAM YARD

SOUTH BASIN

MORICE TOWN

TORPOINT

FERRY

TUNNEL

PUBLIC PARK

DEVONPORT

GUN WHARF

HAMOANE

RAGLAN BARRACKS

DEVONPORT DOCKYARD

FERRY

FERRY

CREMYLL

ROYAL WILLIAM VICT'G YARD

View looking diagonally across South Basin, Keyham yard at the Tower Gates of Albert Road. Incidentally the labour force of the yard was near 4,000, but over the next 20 years increased rapidly to 7,500, due to a massive ship building programme of Battleships and Cruisers.

The Tunnel of 946 yards as indicated joining the two yards was opened in 1857. At first traffic was by horse and cart, but in 1879 a railway line was laid and a light locomotive train was used. Later a footpath was added to one side for pedestrians. Passenger carrying trains were eventually passing through the tunnel and pedestrians had to stand still when the trains passed them, as they would be enveloped in steam and smoke and could fall off the pavement.

A Launch Day, Devonport Dockyards

Launch day in 1904 from No.3 slip South Yard, the vessel was *Hibernia* of 15,360 tons and second in the class to *King Edward VII* which was built and launched in 1902 at Devonport. The Post Card firm made this trial idea of being able to add your photo before sending away, but it didn't really succeed for long.

The ship in the foreground is *Circe*, a training hulk built in 1827 at Devonport, behind is a training hulk and finally *Impregnable*.

It is nice to observe, that the idea of recycling waste is not something new. This local firm took full opportunity to buy up pieces from the Wooden Walled Ships and put the timbers to a more domestic use.

EXCAVATIONS FOR Nº 4 BASIN, 1904.

The greatest extension that Devonport Dockyard had ever experienced, commenced in 1896. About 3,400 men were employed and a new residential district was created at Weston Mill.

The existing engine house and tall chimney are shown here. This area to be known as No.4 Basin had to be dug out of the foreshore area.

Because the mud was so soft for railway trucks, these overhead scoops on overhead cables were erected to clear the mud base, but it wasn't 100% successful.

This view of the North Yard dock's area was originally mud flats and over 4,500,000 cubic yards had to be removed, in some cases 40ft in depth, before a ground base could be established. The granite for the docks came mainly from Cornwall and Norway to a total of 2,500,000 cubic feet. The project cost £6,000,000 and took ten years, but turned Devonport into the biggest Naval Dockyard in Europe, which it still is, despite the great drop-off of work.

HMS *Nile* became portguard ship from 1898-1903 and joined the 4th Division at Devonport until sold in 1912 for £34,900. She was the sister ship to Trafalgar, with a weight of 12,590 tons and had 4 x 13 $\frac{1}{2}$ inch guns. Behind we can observe the covered in No.1 and 2 slipways, a Boat Gear Covered Area, and on the far left, the pit and props of No.3 slipway.

A domestic view of Cremyll Beach, with passenger ferries on the foreshore. In the background is a dredger, and the fine granite structure of South Yard

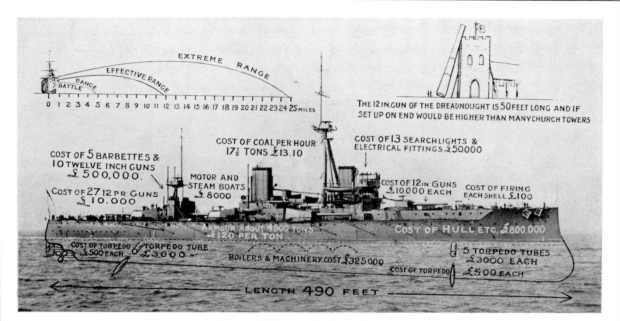

Facts and Figures of a 'Dreadnought'

A 'Dreadnought' costs £2,000,000 to build. The diagram shows how the money is spent, and the size and range of the ten 12 inch guns. The total pay of the 'Dreadnought's' officers and men is nearly £1,000 a week, and the cost of government rations is more than £200 a week. If lying in Dover harbour the 'Dreadnought' from her ten 12 inch guns can easily drop huge shells, weighing 850lbs, into the town of Calais, across the Straights of Dover, or from the mouth of the Thames below Gravesend, can shell the Tower of London.

HMS *Warspite*, the most famous Devonport built warship, completed in 1915, weight 31,100 tons and showing 8 in No, 15 inch guns and 16 in No, 6 inch guns.

Shown here before her 3rd refit, she was badly damaged at the Battle of Jutland, but attended the German surrender. In the second world war, she was involved at Narvick, Matapan, and Normandy, but in 1946 was sold for breaking up. Finally, early 1947 when under tow for the Clyde, she parted the tow along the Cornish coast, ran aground at Prussia Cove and became a tourist attraction. In 1950 she was refloated but beached again off Marazion, and the breaking up and scrapping continued until 1956.

HMS *Minotaur* being launched at Devonport in 1906, from the newly made slip. This class of WATTS' ARMOURED Cruiser 14,600 tons was the third group of 3 and the last in his design, presented one of the most ferocious sights in the fleet. There were 4 large funnels, 4 in No, 9.2 inch guns (2 fwd and 2 aft) and port and starboard rows of 5 in No, 7.5 inch guns (total 10). She came through the Jutland affair un-scathed and her cost was £1,400,000.

The small original Royal Sailors Rest outside Fore St Gate, and the larger grand building, which was the original sight of the three public houses. 'Napier', 'Royal Naval Rendezvous' and 'Dock Gates Inn', which Miss Agnes Weston bought and rebuilt to her requirements by 1912. Her ambition was to buy Gamlen Brothers Corner and other properties (to the left and out of the picture). After her sudden death in 1918, a donation of £30,000 was made by admirers to build this block as a memorial to a fine lady.

Part of the structure of the 160 ton electric revolving cantilever crane to be built east side of the Prince of Wales Basin in 1907. Messrs Cowans Sheldon & Co of Carlisle supplied the crane.

The main support frame work being built, by using (shown here) one of three lattice-work wooden pillar supports, each of 50ft high with a platform on top. This assist framework was supplied by Butters Bros of Glasgow and a steam crane was mounted on top. The crane was completed in 1909 and worked until 1978, when it was made redundant, and subsequently dismantled by Dockyard Boilermakers.

A re-tubing squad of Boilermakers at Devonport in 1915. This trade was normally a very dirty job as most of the work was done by hand. Their working clothes were coat and trousers of a very heavy canvas, very stout boots, and the traditional flat hat of the general workforce at that period. They could have also been involved in work erecting the Cantilever Crane, with riveting structure etc.

The Admiralty Yacht *Vivid* seen here with the Prince of Wales on board, entering the North Lock, leading into the main enclosed basin in 1907. The occasion being the opening of the complete area of Docks (shown insert above) which then made Devonport the best equipped and largest war-port in the world. This lock could also be used for docking down ships.

Looking up through the length of the Lock many years later, i.e. 1969 we see HMS *Penelope* docked down. The following year work commenced to build a dividing wall midway. In 1972 these two new docks No.11 and No.12 were flooded and used for nuclear fleet submarine and conventional subs. Also any other vessels that would have normally docked in 5, 6 and 7 which were currently out of use due to the New Frigate Complex work. In case of a National emergency, should the main basin caisson become jammed, the dividing wall could be blown out, thus allowing the ships in the 3 major docks to leave via the old Lock method.

A fine collection of the work force in the early 1920's, posing for Dockyard photographers. They appear to be sitting in front of the riveted side of a caisson, and are graded with the bowler hatted bosses at the front. The Shipwrights are amongst the lower groups, but the rest are drillers, riveters and men with dolly punches and of course the rivet boys.

Britains New Navy in Training
H.M.S. RALEIGH

A look into the various activities of the new rating entering the Navy at the shore establishment inland from Torpoint in 1953.
Raleigh was recognised as being the stoker training school, with HMS Fisguard across the road for Artificer Training Apprentices.

H. M. S. "Hibernia" (1st. Class Battleship. 16 350 tons.)

THE TRIUMPH OF THE TWELVE APOSTLES

Vice-Admiral Lord Charles Beresford, was, in the early 1900's, the Commander-in-Chief of the famous Channel Fleet. When the *Hibernia* – Charlie's flagship – was commissioned at Devonport, a signal was made to challenge all ships for a five mile race in twelve-oared cutters for any amount of money that their opponents would care to put up. On this occasion, to everyone's amazement, and to the joy of the ship's company, a dockyard matey came aboard and asked to see the coxswain of the racing cutter, as he thought he had a crew of dockyard matey's that might accept the challenge. The coxswain asked the 'Dockyardee' if it was a joke or was he really serious. The dockyard matey assured him that he was never more serious in his life.

The stake money was being guaranteed by the landlord of the 'Two Trees', a noted pub in Fore Street, Devonport, who, he said, was prepared to back them up to £300 – a very large sum in those days.

Both boats were towed out to the Breakwater and excitement was at fever pitch throughout the fleet. At the starting-buoy, both cutters edged up into line, the gun fired and they were off.

As the *Hibernia*'s boat approached the turn around Drake's Island, she looked like a man trying to run whilst sunk up to his knees in treacle. She was making hardly any headway at all, although her crew were pulling their hearts out. This was because they had struck against the full force of the vicious tide which at certain times sweeps around the Island.

The Twelve Apostles' (a nickname given by the navy) coxswain had learnt all about such tides by bitter experience, this shot him and his crew around the island and home at a speed which the *Hibernia*'s boat had never attained in all their previous races.

What a triumph it was for the Twelve Apostles, who apparently every day except Sundays with their cutter would gently emerge from the dockyard steps at 7.30a.m., and row out to the Breakwater in Plymouth Sound, where the crew would carry out their daily quota of painting, patching and cementing necessary to keep the Breakwater in good trim. Then, at the end of their day's work, they would stow their gear and row back to the Dockyard, so they knew the tides.

A Boat's Crew.

During the earlier 1900's this would have been the daily scene of the men going aboard for the day, and having their boxes stowed aboard, near to the job. Tea making was carried out ashore using Dockside wood burning boilers at the appropriate times.

In the latter years canteens were established and now individual lockers are provided plus washbasins, showers etc to bring the system further up to date.

A Staff Paymaster, who after passing Civil Service exams enters the Navy as assistant clerk at 2s-6d a day and as Paymaster in Chief who will receive 38s a day. The Gold Cord indicates that the wearer is secretary to a Flag Officer.

HMS *Orion* with her large displacement of 22,200 tons and the class, were regarded as 'Super Dreadnoughts'. They were the first to carry all their heavy guns in centre line turrets. The class of 4, survived Jutland, and in 1917 were fitted with take off platforms for scout aircraft of top of 'B' turret. Launched in 1910 she is seen here at Devonport being manouvered by tugs for the Breakers Yard journey in 1922.

The Quadrangle Building overlooking No.3 Basin during 1930, when crane tracks were being progressed further for future large steam cranes. These sheer legs remained until the mid 1950's (Book 3 Page 8).
Note the iron wheeled lorries by the Quadrangle and Goose Neck Crane just past the sheer legs. Identity of Warship unfortunately not known.

Draught of Water over Sill when Docked.	No. of Dock.	SHIP.	When Docked.	When Undocked.	Draught of Water when Docked. Forward.	Draught of Water when Docked. Aft.	Draught of Water when Undocked. Forward.	Draught of Water when Undocked. Aft.	Description of any Special Works Performed. Certificate that Draught Marks are Correct.	Signatures of Officers, &c, concerned. Draughtsman for Certificate of Draught Marks; Assistant Constructor or Foreman of the Yard for all other Information.
1.	2.	3	4	5	6	7	8	9	10	11
15-6 13-0	Shallow	"Torres"	24·3·31 1000	8·4·31 0805	4-3	8-0	4-0	8-0	Docking & Defects.	R. Bishop
34-0 43-6		"Norfolk"	1·4·31 1400	23·4·31 1000	14-9	19-10	19-10	19-10	Annual Docking & G.O.B.	F. Emmet
26-0 12-0		"The D56"	2·4·31 1040	30·4·31 1415	13-5	14-6	3-0	14-3	Docking & Defects.	F. Gibson.
31-0 over	5	"Exeter"	2·4·31 1045	23·4·31 1630	14-0	14-6	14-1	13-2	Examⁿ W.W. Fittings & C.O.B. preparatory to Sea Trials	C.H. Mitchell
32-0	8	"Malaya"	30·3·31 1625	29·4·31 1455	28-4	26-5½	28-3	28-5	Repairs to damaged Stem	W.R. Brown

A typical page from the Dockyard Docking Book D302, during 1931. Docking down a ship is a very complex job, especially if she is in for a long refit. During 1928 there were 139 dockings. During 1928 there were 139 dockings, 1938-170 and prior to the war 1939-213, 1966-170 and now with such a reduced Navy the numbers are very low indeed. During 1944, there were 193, of which 82 were U.S. Land ship Tank craft, coming in for the same repair, damaged propellers or stern tubes.

One of the last Direct current Electric Goose Neck cranes, on the sea wall, north of 'R' caisson, during the mid 1960's.

In the foreground are two donkey boilers, i.e. Stationery Steam Engines used on the dockside by the Navy to give steam heating to vessels under going refit work.

A collection of cranes in the Prince of Wales Basin area, by the main 'R' caisson entrance, on the southern end. From left to right we have a Goose neck crane, a Pile Driver Structure working on the Basin Wall, a Travelling portable electric Tower Crane, a dockside diesel crane and the largest, a floating crane in the river, shown here around the 1929's.

COPYRIGHT. ABRAHAMS.   911   H.M. SUBMARINE "L 1."   DEVONPORT

Due to the keeness of this photographer at the time, we can now look at such rare comparisons of vessels. A line up of wooden walled hulks which formed the training establishment mid stream, and a modern underwater submarine L1. She was built 1917 and broken up in 1930. She had a 3 inch gun on a disappearing mounting, plus 18 inch torpedoes.

From
Abrahams & Sons,
NAVAL PHOTOGRAPHERS,
4 MARLBOROUGH STREET,
DEVONPORT

Copyright 2423   THE HAMOAZE, DEVONPORT HARBOUR.   Abrahams, Devonport

A rather quiet impression of the River and part of the Dockyard with a Destroyer, Aircraft Carrier, possibly the *Eagle*, and a Battleship anchored mid stream. Note the buildings and approaches near to the jetty for the Torpoint Ferry and foreground space.

HIORNS & MILLER

SUCCESSORS

THE

NAVY. ARMY.

& AIR FORCE.

PHONE – 437 DEVONPORT.

GRAMS HIORNS-MIL DEVONPO

PRINTERS & STATIONERS.

DEVONPORT.

107. FORE STREET.

These are firm's that supplied and served the Navy and Dockyard employee's and advertised in their magazines and Navy day programmes.

SPOONERS

AT YOUR SERVICE

The Departmental Store of the West

What a wilderness Plymouth would be

without

POPHAMS

and

THE NAVY

Bedford Street Plymouth   *Telephone 803*

Erebus, one of two Monitors built in 1916 and designed to carry a modern British armament of two 15 inch guns, 8 in No 4 inch and 2 in No 3 inch guns. In 1917 was struck by an electrically controlled motor boat, and 1918 was hit by bombs during an air raid at Dunkirk.
She was later converted to a Turret Drill ship, with accommodation and served at Devonport during 1927-1928.

HMS *Centurion*, a King George V class Battleship of 23,000 tons was built at Devonport in 1911 and completed 1913. Served in the Battle of Jutland, and later was converted into a Target ship and was Radio Controlled by the Destroyer *Shikari*. In 1941, at Devonport she was disguised with paint, canvas and plywood to represent the Battleship *Anson* in order to deceive the *Axis* in the Mediterranean. The job was estimated to take a month, but it had to be carried out in 2 weeks, which was accomplished by working day and night.

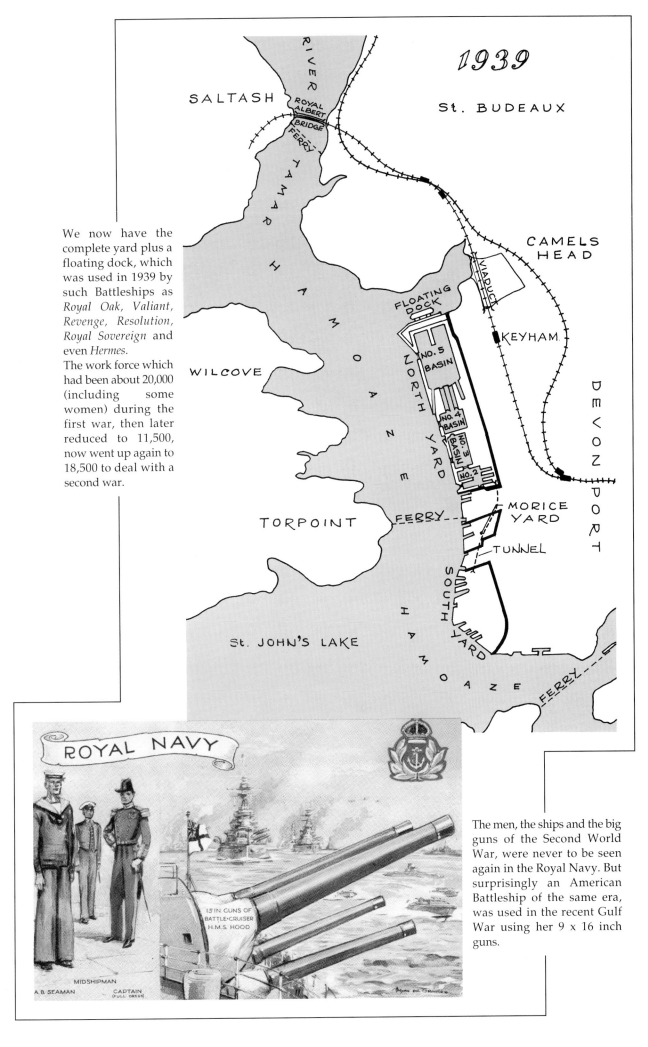

1939

SALTASH   RIVER   ROYAL ALBERT BRIDGE   FERRY   St. BUDEAUX

T A M A R

We now have the complete yard plus a floating dock, which was used in 1939 by such Battleships as *Royal Oak, Valiant, Revenge, Resolution, Royal Sovereign* and even *Hermes.*

The work force which had been about 20,000 (including some women) during the first war, then later reduced to 11,500, now went up again to 18,500 to deal with a second war.

WILCOVE

H A M O A Z E

CAMELS HEAD

VIADUCT

FLOATING DOCK

NO. 5 BASIN

NO. 4 BASIN

NO. 3 BASIN

NO. 2

NORTH YARD

KEYHAM

D E V O N P O R T

MORICE YARD

TUNNEL

SOUTH YARD

TORPOINT   FERRY

St. JOHN'S LAKE

H A M O A Z E

FERRY

ROYAL NAVY

15 IN. GUNS OF BATTLE-CRUISER H.M.S. HOOD

MIDSHIPMAN

A.B. SEAMAN   CAPTAIN (FULL DRESS)

The men, the ships and the big guns of the Second World War, were never to be seen again in the Royal Navy. But surprisingly an American Battleship of the same era, was used in the recent Gulf War using her 9 x 16 inch guns.

HMS *Ramillies* one of the famous 'R' class Battleships, under camouflage netting whilst in No.10 dock during 1942. Many large dockside steam cranes can be seen and a ship's funnel laying on its side. High on the sky line is the 160 ton Cantilver crane on the east side of the P.O.W. Basin. The tall building behind this crane was the Heavy Turnery, where submarine shafts, gun barrels and similar work could be turned on large lathes.

Here *Ramillies* seen in the floating dock, and note the ship side anti Torpedo bulge, which had been added, which gave problems to entering some dry docks. She was built 1917 and scrapped 1948.

Fore Street Gate, South Yard, at night. Suitably decorated to
celebrate the Coronation year 1953 of Queen Elizabeth II.

Ferry Road Gate, at the intersection of New Passage Hill and Ferry Road, this gate also displayed
Royal Decorations. It is one of the few gates that hasn't changed over the years, but takes more
motor traffic now with its recent large car park built to the rear of these steps and bushes.

THE AIRCRAFT CARRIER Glorious arriving at Plymouth
from the Mediterranean station. She is to be refitted at a cost
of about £200,000.

Courageous, Glorious and *Furious* were built in 1916 as Battleships, but were all later in the 1920's
given to Devonport for conversion into Aircraft Carriers. *Glorious* herself was a gunners school ship
at Devonport before her conversion. Seen here arriving at Devonport before the Second War for a
minor refit. She was eventually sunk by gunfire in 1940 by the German *Scharnhorst* and *Gneisenau*.

HMAS *Sydney* was handed over to the Royal Australian Navy in 1948. Originally built in
Devonport Dockyard and launched in 1944 from No.3 Slipway, South Yard, with the name HMS
Terrible. Displacement 14,000 tons and was finally broken up in 1975.

HMS *Vulcan*, built 1889 as a Torpedo Boat Cruiser, shown passing across the Sound on the way to the breakers in 1955. She was a new design experiment, had two funnels and either side of the after funnel was fitted with 2 large cranes. These were for launching and stowing the 6 Torpedo Boats she carried.

Her later years were spent as part of HMS *Defiance* along with *Inconstant* and *Andromeda*.

Automatic Twin 3 inch Gun Turret, similar to the trial turrets used on HMS *Cumberland* and finally fitted on the Tiger/Blake Cruisers. These were designed to fire 120 rounds/min, but actually found it more practical at 90 rounds.

Shown here on the cast iron wheeled low loader outside the Fore Street Gate in 1960.

The buildings behind housed the M.C.D Drawing Office until 1966, when they were moved to the new Central Office Block inside Albert Road Gate area.

Horses were used for at least 260 years in the Dockyard, and were finally phased out in 1960. This Government Contractor, John Hitchins and Co., operated from the stables under the Union Street Railway Arches – near the New Leisure Complex area. During 1925 horses could be seen working alongside steam wagons, railway trains and motor vehicles.

Engine No.1 in 1902, hauled a royal train carrying King Edward VII and Queen Alexandra who had visited the yard to lay a keel plate of his namesake Battleship. The train then transported them to the Naval Barracks, and thus the Royal Coat of Arms was displayed.

Engine No.19 is still hauling passenger coaches at the Bodmin Steam Railway preserved line, after being refurbished by enthusiasts.

The last run of the steam hauled passenger train service in the Dockyard, May 1966, seen here at South Yard, with the Tower Cranes of the main building slip looking on. It has been said that 13 million passengers were transported over the 19 miles of railway system during its lifetime.

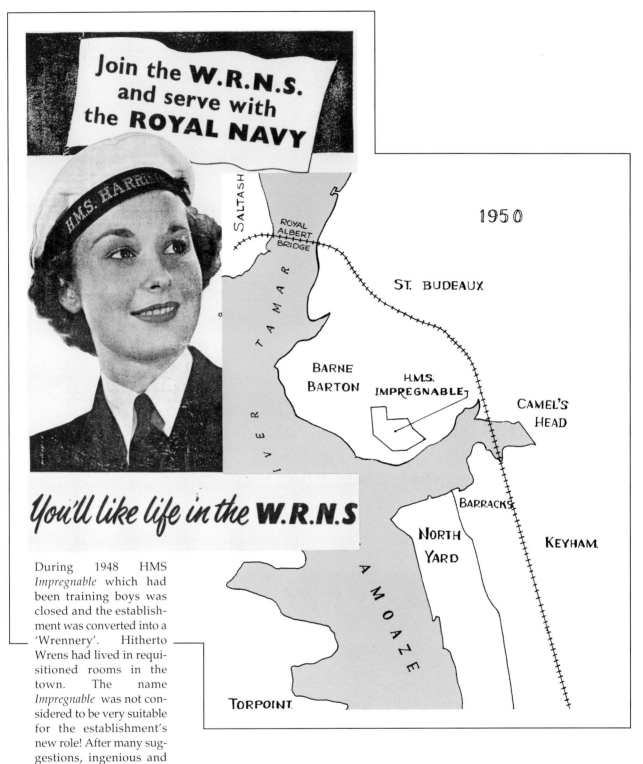

Join the **W.R.N.S.** and serve with the **ROYAL NAVY**

You'll like life in the **W.R.N.S**

SALTASH

ROYAL ALBERT BRIDGE

RIVER TAMAR

1950

ST. BUDEAUX

BARNE BARTON

H.M.S. IMPREGNABLE

CAMEL'S HEAD

BARRACKS

NORTH YARD

HAMOAZE

KEYHAM.

TORPOINT.

During 1948 HMS *Impregnable* which had been training boys was closed and the establishment was converted into a 'Wrennery'. Hitherto Wrens had lived in requisitioned rooms in the town. The name *Impregnable* was not considered to be very suitable for the establishment's new role! After many suggestions, ingenious and otherwise had been turned down, the establishment was named 'St Budeaux Wrens Quarters'.

Unknown to these Wrens, their washroom activities were being monitored by hot blooded Dockyard men, using ships Binoculars or Gun Telescopes from ships berthed in the North Corner of the main Basin.

Now during 1990, Wrens have at last been given the opportunity to serve aboard a fighting ship – HMS *Brilliant* being the first.

An artist's impression of one of the 'Old Brigade of 1919' Boilermakers. The brushes shown are a pair of de-scaling brushes which he would push up the boiler tubes to remove the scale, which collects after a lot of steaming. What he would have thought of the situation below, I dread to think, throwing a Dockyard Boiler around!

"Fallen off the back of a Lorry" is an expression often used. But here we see the sad affect of HMS Scylla's boiler, which was going to be installed on the slipway (a first time arrangement) in 1968. The contractors lorry was instructed to drive out through St Levans Gate, along St Levens Road to Milehouse and around to South Yard, but at the last minute he thought he would save time, and turned sharp right up the hill past the College, the resulting top heavy load didn't agree and thus parted company.

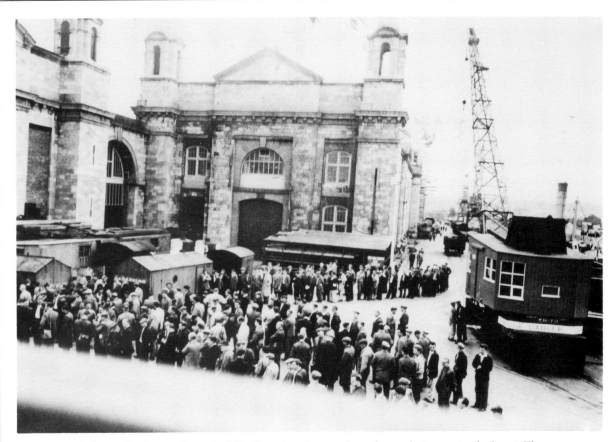

A domestic view at the end of the day, showing yard employees lining up to clock out. The area shown is the North West corner of the Boiler Shop, adjacent to No.3 North Basin during 1958. Note the dockside diesel crane, and tower mobile cranes further along.

At the South West corner of the Quadrangle, about the same period and time of day. Inside this corner of the building was the Heavy Turnery Shop. Note the various hand carts and other dockside lumber, this corner is now occupied by the Frigate Complex.

Multiple building of barges on the main building slip South Yard. These store barges for the Captain Port Engineer were built in 1967, in a slack building period. This was later changed to R.M.A.S. Control and these barges were then used at Faslane.

Ship building was becoming slack, with only 6 frigates between 1953-1968 against 10 Battleships, 2 Battle Cruisers and 3 Cruisers between 1900-1914.

In total the yard during its 300 years has built 308 ships, ranging from Wooden Wallers, Battleships, Cruisers, Submarines, Frigates, Floating Docks, some Merchant Ships and one Aircraft Carrier.

This overall view from the Tidal Basin at Keyham, looks across to *Ark Royal* docked down in No.10 dock during its 1969 refit. The *Ark* and *Eagle* were regular visitors to the yard, with *Eagle* having a 4 year refit from 1960, and *Ark* in 1959, 1961, and then in 1966 for a 3 year £30 million modernisation to enable Phantom aircraft to be used. Note the projections from flight deck to recover bridle loops. During this refit was added 300 tons of flight deck plating, 1,200 miles of electric cable, 450 tons of paint and 18 miles of piping for water systems. *Ark Royal* was launched in 1950 by the Queen Mother and accepted by the Royal Navy in 1955 at a cost of £21,428,000. In the foreground of view we can see the water carrier *Fresh Pond*, *Alsatian* a diesel tug, *Director* the diesel electric paddle tug, and the after end of *Superman* the steam paddle tug.

This unusual item was built on No.3 slip way in 1971, and was named *Crystal*. She was a Research and Development floating laboratory for use in Portland. Shown here receiving one of the frameworks for lowering down through a hole in the hull to test acoustic equipment. The vessel had no engines, rudder or armament, so she was towed all the way to Portland.

HMS *Penelope*, a Leander Class Frigate built 1962, shown in dry dock at Devonport she is the 11th ship to bear this name, and in 1982 she had a refit to install an Exocet Missle System and a Lynx Helicopter. Now this year she has been sold to the Ecuador Government along with HMS *Danae*.

The 'Cod War' incident in 1973, when the Royal Navy was involved with Icelandic Gun Boats over fishing rights. This unfortunately led to some Leander Class Frigates becoming damaged. Here in the dry dock at Devonport is HMS *Leander* with substantial under water damage. She had to have 19ft of her bow removed and replaced.

This scale model of the Frigate Complex was made in the Mould Loft in the early 1970's to prove that all ships of the Navy's future Frigates would fit the docks. Unfortunately a few years after the actual Complex was opened, a new idea to lengthen future ships by approximately 25ft was made, consequently the Complex was no longer usable.

An aerial photo of the Complex during the building programme, showing the temporary road way and detailed structure of this Triple Garage for the Navy. During the late 1980's, the centre dock had to be extended out into the basin area, to cater for the new length of Frigates. The Complex on completion was opened by Foreign Secretary Dr David Owen, M.P., and cost approx £16,000,000. This allows 24 hour working in controlled conditions, with administration offices, workshops, washing facilities etc all under one roof per ship.

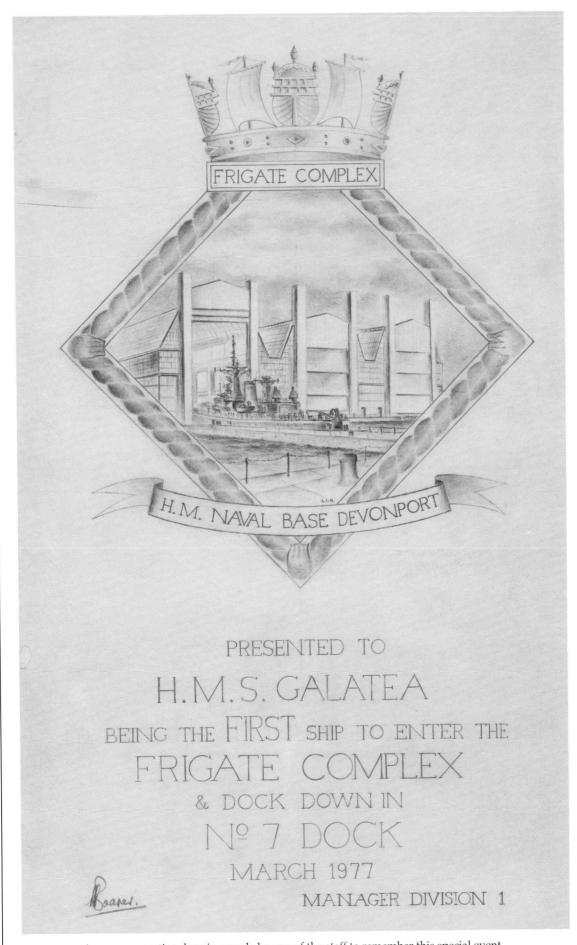

FRIGATE COMPLEX

H.M. NAVAL BASE DEVONPORT

PRESENTED TO

H.M.S. GALATEA

BEING THE FIRST SHIP TO ENTER THE

FRIGATE COMPLEX

& DOCK DOWN IN

No 7 DOCK

MARCH 1977

MANAGER DIVISION 1

A commemorative drawing made by one of the staff to remember this special event. Remembering of course that in 1853 in this same area, No.3 dock as it was then called, a similar event took place, when HMS *Queen* was the first ship to enter the dock, fully manned on the yard arms, for the opening, it was in future called Queen's Dock.

The two largest Carriers in the Royal Navy shown here with *Ark Royal* passing *Eagle* having just completed a Dockyard refit. *Eagle* went for scrap in 1978.

The public was introduced to the *Ark Royal* through a BBC TV series called 'Sailor', giving life aboard the great floating airfield, also introduced was the Navy version of 'Magic Roundabout' and Rod Stewart's song 'Sailing'.

During ten months aboard a 1960 commission the crew of 2000 ate, 15 miles of sausages, consumed 125,000 pints of beer, smoked 12,500,000 cigarettes 3,655 cigars and 7,664 ozs of tobacco. The wages over the same period totalled £400,000. This would be quite a contract for firms to get again, but sadly these big ships are gone forever.

The Scrieve Board, South yard alongside No.3 slip as it was called in the 19th century, here ships lines and sections are marked out on the wooden floor, full size, for shipwrights and blacksmiths to make moulds for bending frames and plate work.

View of the Scrieve Board, from the river, and note 'the prop and job hoists' shown above, were replaced in 1972, with a 'Goliath' travelling 3 tons crane, such was the difference of work from earlier Battleships, to small refits on RAF Launches. Underneath the Scrieve Board is still the original slipway No.4.

The Mine Counter Measures Vessel, normally with wooden hulls, has moved into the plastic world. This is the World's largest Aluminium Female Mould, 60 metres long, 10 metres wide, and draught 2.5 metres. Built in Devonport, being the only place capable to undertake such as task in 1974. The hull consists of 16 units on Castor Frameworks, these were transported to Vospers – Southampton and re-assembled. Using overhead travellers, layers of Cloth impregnated in resin were laid on the inside to a thickness of 35mm. When cured, the sections were rolled away leaving the ships hull.

HMS *Cottesmore*, one of the 'Tupperware' ships made from this mould. During the 1991 Gulf War it was quoted the R.N. were using their most advanced and expensive ships, full of British Electronics to sweep the seas before the big attack. The little ships with the biggest job.

DEVONPORT. FORE STREET, 46/47.

This shows what was a busy shopping street, leading down to the Fore Street Dockyard Gate as it was in 1947. This area has now been taken over by the Dockyard and the 3 buildings – namely Marks and Spencers, a Bank and Burtons – are still there, being used as stores. The nissen huts were introduced when the American troops arrived and were used for many more years.

North Corner, Devonport

North Corner about 1910, has since had a fly-over built, from beside the tall building across to the left hand edge of the view. Thus joining up Morice Yard to South Yard by internal road-way. Morice Yard was joined to Keyham by a flyover on the Ferry Road. This was the reason for the steam passenger train service to finish in 1966. A replacement Bus Service followed, using these new bridges making the the Yard one long establishment approx. 2.5 miles.

Going Up! This large project the 'Submarine Refit Complex' started in 1973 and was opened by the Prince of Wales in 1980. It consists of 2 large Nuclear Sub Docks, Admin Blocks, Workshops and support facilities. The most prominent feature is the large 80 tonne crane, seen here still having its Jib, and control mechanisms yet to be built.

Going Down! The Royal Navy Engineering College, Keyham in 1985, after 105 years work, was being pulled down as no longer required. It was the Naval Training Establishment for the Officer Class of the System. In 1950 the Dockyard used the facilities, for a Devonport Dockyard Technical College, capable of housing 1,500 apprentices.
Now the site holds a block of square shaped portakabins for M.O.D.(N) office workers.

No.1 slip, beside 'King Billy', built in 1763, was later covered in, by designer Richard Perrin in 1814. Later all the slipways were covered in bar one. In those early wooden ship building days, ships built in the open, were prematurely decaying whilst on the slip, and consequently would only last 6-7 years.

These roofs were originally covered by making the canopy of deals and covering with tarred paper, and estimated to cost £10,000, but was said at the time, the ships would last for 200 years being built in the dry.

This re-roofing work done in 1991, consists of timber planks, roofing tarred paper, and finally aluminium sheeting, with the addition of aluminium framed windows.

It is often said the History repeats itself. Here we have in 1814 the idea of covered in slipways, and some docks, to protect the timber from rotting. Now in 1977 we have a covered Dock Complex (see page 50) to protect the men, and materials and allow for 24 hour shift working.

The main gate to the Royal Navy Barracks situated at the North End of the Dockyard area, which celebrated its 100th anniversary in 1989. This main approach to the training area has not altered at all, only its activities within. Inshore establishments HMS *Raleigh* and for a time *Fisguard, near* Torpoint are the centres now for the raw recruit entries.

'A GIRL IN EVERY PORT'
TO GREET YOU!

Jack was and always will be the subject of being the romantic cavalier of the seas. Of course in the early part of this century, he would be away for 2 year commissions, which would breed his wonderlust. But now the modern navy has reduced its time away, to help combat this.

Devonport has been noted since 1907, for its Naval Field Gun Crew Displays. It's now one of the main features of the annual Royal Tournament at Earls Court. It's the transfer of a field gun, across a simulated chasm, through a narrow gap, and to re-build the gun for action. Here you can see a pair of wheels being transferred. The wooden wheels are maintained and rebuilt where necessary by dockyard Wheelwrights.

Navy Days, the annual show piece for the public to see the ships and meet the men. River activities are always popular, as the helicopter display shows. Unfortunately with so many people on one side of the ships at once, it can become increasingly dangerous for the ships stability, as it did one year.
Sadly as from 1991, Navy Days will be bi-annually commencing with Devonport as the only yard open, then Portsmouth in 1992.

Jack ashore at an Art Gallery, giving himself a visual reminder of the maritime hero – Nelson – trying to imagine the Battle of Trafalgar that has been recorded, and wondering whether he will be really called to do his duty for the Country in actual Naval Warfare and how he will re-act.

Here we see the 'Future Navy' on parade at Stonehouse Barracks in 1990, being represented by the Royal Marine Volunteer Cadet Corps and the Sea Cadets.

Quite recently the Navy has finally allowed W.R.N.S. to serve aboard a fighting warship, and not just to be trained for shore establishment activities.

More staff needed but axe will still fall

David Johnston (right) speaking at the press conference. On the left is managing director Mike Leece.

DEVONPORT Dockyard's new team today launched a campaign to take on about 170 workers to cope with privatisation.

The move comes despite an announcement that 2,300 posts will be axed at the complex during the next four years.

The new openings are for 150 unskilled industrial workers and up to 20 specialist white collar staff.

Devonport Management Limited, the consortium led by U.S.-owned Brown and Root, say they are the key to a "more commercial approach."

DML's deputy chairman David Johnston, the complex's former Civil Service managing director, said: "These are entirely new jobs.

"They are important as we are starting to build up in commercial areas."

The white collar staff will be engaged in negotiating and drawing up contracts and giving estimates for outside work.

And today, on the first day of privatisation, DML clashed with the Defence Ministry over £2-million worth of "guaranteed" work.

The new managers were furious when the Government tried to remove a string of weapons overhauls from the complex just hours before they took over.

A series of sharply worded telexes flew between the Yard and Whitehall forcing the Ministry to pledge further talks on its plans.

New managing director Mike Leece, said: "Our reaction was one of surprise. I am certain it is a hiccup in the system and will not happen again."

The Government also told DML it was temporarily cutting back on Devonport's lucrative nuclear submarine refit work.

However, it offered to give the firm six extra ship overhauls to do at Devonport to compensate.

Mr Johnston described the move as "a bonus."

A sad day for the city, says Lord Mayor

THE DOCKYARD GOES PRIVATE

by **MICHAEL JOHNSTON**
Industry reporter

PRIVATE MANAGERS today took over control of Devonport Dockyard for the first time in its 300-year history.

Vesting Day, as the Government has called the official switch to privatisation, was the day many have fought long and hard against.

One worker, express-

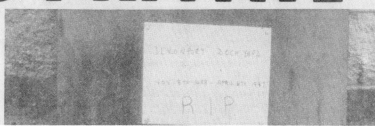

APRIL 6 – 1987
THE NEW TASK

The Dockyard has been used to doing major conversion work to ships during its M.O.D.(N) career.

Now D.M.L. have a big self conversion task, to change this M.O.D. Shire Horse labour force, with its capacity to take on any tasks, so be it taking its time, but with no task being too big, and always reliable to complete in the end.

To – A Slimmer Style Racehorse, with the potential of getting to the finishing post on time, with the ability to win business for its new owners. Also with its new streamlined style, becoming the favourite in all big tasks available on the open markets of jobs.

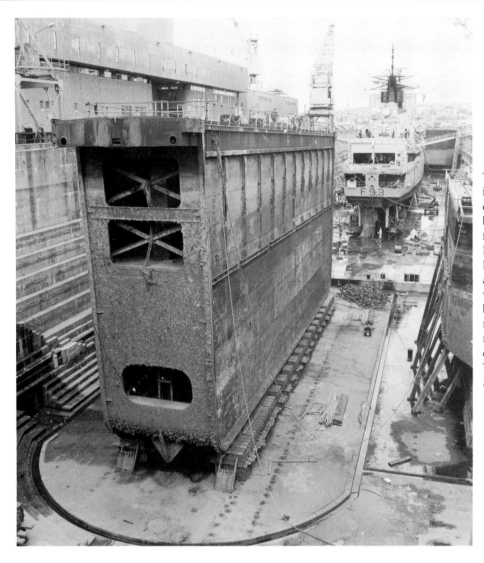

This is the biggest caisson in the dockyard and fits the entrance at 'R' position, being the only opening from the river into the Prince O' Wales Basin. The Dockyard built it in 1924 and it is 136ft long, 20ft wide and 55ft high. The biggest task will be to remove generations of barnacles and marine growth during this refit in 1990. The ship behind is HMS *Beaver*.

Shipwrights can be seen hammering oakum into the seams, whilst the other man is boiling pitch using a burning torch. When oakum is well packed, the hot pitch is applied, to make the joint water tight.

On a Battleship where appearance was necessary, after pitch was hardened, a pneumatic planing machine, (like a lawn mower) was used to plane the area flush. The Navy in turn at sea used to scrub the wood decks with a type of hearth stone (this was known as 'Holystoning the Deck').

The first of the British Steel Challenge Yachts being built in No.3 Shop. South Yard. Devonport Management Limited (D.M.L.) has obtained a contract to build eleven such yachts from 1990 onwards.

H.R.H. the Princess Royal named the first yacht and Chay Blythe attended with some of the Volunteer crews that would eventually sail in the yachts to come.

These crews have signed up for the eight month match race around the World, scheduled to start Oct 1992.

Music for the occasion was provided by the Royal Marine Band, with traditional Devon Cream Teas being served from a large marquee. Congratulations D.M.L. it was done in grand style.

AN INTERCITY 125 HIGH SPEED TRAIN
CROSSING THE TAMAR

It's a hat-trick! D.M.L. Diesels has simultaneously won three contracts, totalling over £15 million, in open and fierce competition. Two of the contracts have been awarded by B.R.B. (British Railways Board) and the other by the M.O.D. as part of their S.M.R. (Stock, Maintenance and Repair) programme.

The first B.R.B. contract will bring about 30 Paxman Valenta power units (used in Inter City 125 high speed trains) in for overhaul each year.

The M.O.D. contract, (which is for Stock, Maintenance and Repair work) is for the overhaul of 50 Paxman Ventura diesel engines, which are fitted in Type 21 and Type 22 frigates.

NOTE. It is very ironic that 300 years after Saltash said *No* to a Dockyard as it would destroy their livelihood. Now the Yard has captured work from trains that pass over the same river area.